Joseph Battell

Vermont illustrated

Supplement of the Middlebury Register

Joseph Battell

Vermont illustrated
Supplement of the Middlebury Register

ISBN/EAN: 9783741146626

Manufactured in Europe, USA, Canada, Australia, Japa

Cover: Foto ©Thomas Meinert / pixelio.de

Manufactured and distributed by brebook publishing software
(www.brebook.com)

Joseph Battell

Vermont illustrated

JANUARY 7, 1898.

VERMONT ILLUSTRATED.

SUPPLEMENT OF

THE MIDDLEBURY REGISTER

Middlebury, Vermont.

SUPPLEMENT OF

THE MIDDLEBURY REGISTER,

JANUARY 7, 1898.

PRINTED BY
THE REGISTER COMPANY,
MIDDLEBURY, VERMONT.

VERMONT ILLUSTRATED.

VERMONT is an eminently picturesque state. While it lacks that sublimity of natural scenery that marks the loftiest mountains, the deepest canons and the mightiest cataracts, it presents a variety of landscape and forest, hill, valley and plain, thriving farm and green-clad mountain, shining river and rushing brook, so infinite and ever changing as to afford the traveler a constant series of pleasant surprises. It is, by comparison, but a little state, lying between the parallels 42°, 44', and 45° north, and the longitude 3°, 35' and 5°, 20' east from Washington. Its north boundary on the Province of Quebec is 90 miles long, whence the state narrows in breadth to 41 miles at its southern border on Massachusetts. The length is 158 miles, and it lies between the Connecticut River on the east and the state of New York on the west—the west boundary running through Lake Champlain east of the "Four Brothers" and west of Grand Isle and Isle La Motte. The eastern boundary is 215 and the western 175 miles. The state is divided into fourteen counties, containing 245 towns. The area is a little over 10,000 square miles. The longest day on the south line of the state is 15 hours, 9 minutes and 9 seconds, and at the north line 15 hours, 25 minutes and 50 seconds.   The north line upon the parallel of latitude 45 north was first surveyed by commissioners of the provinces of New York and Canada in 1767.   The eastern boundary was established by a decree of George III., July 20, 1764, which declared the western bank of the Connecticut river to be the western boundary of New Hampshire.   The southern boundary is derived from a royal decree of March 4, 1740, but, it is said, was erroneously surveyed from allowance of too great a variation in the magnetic needle, through which New Hampshire lost 59,873 acres and Vermont 133,897, and the south line of Vermont is not parallel with the north line.   The western boundary was settled by Vermont and New York in 1790.

The Green Mountain range enters the state at its southern boundary and extends northerly through its entire length, dividing the state into nearly equal parts.   But in the southern part of Washington county the range divides into two branches, the higher of which continues, a little east of north, along the eastern lines of Chittenden and Franklin counties, into Canada; while the other tends much more to the east through the southern and eastern parts of Washington, the western part of Caledonia and the northwestern part of Essex county, to Canada.   Through the first of these branches, in which rises Mount Mansfield, 4,279 feet (called the highest peak in the state), the Winooski, Lamoille and Missisquoi rivers penetrate, along whose banks are excellent roads and magnificent scenery.   The eastern branch, having no peaks so high, is more uniformly elevated.   It is called the "height of land," and divides the waters that fall into Connecticut River, in the north part of the state, from those that find their way to Lakes Champlain and Memphremagog.   This range continues in Canada near the south side of the St. Lawrence River to the gulf, near which are several peaks measuring about 4,000 feet.   The Taconic range, which enters the south part of the state near the western border, extends northward into Addison county, where it ends.   It forms the western boundary of the valley of Otter Creek up to that point.   This range is particularly noteworthy from the fact that in its mountains are found all of the valuable deposits of marble which have made the state famous for that product.

Among the more notable mountains not before mentioned are Camel's Hump in Huntington, Chittenden county, 4,183 feet; Potato Hill and Bread Loaf Mountain, in Addison county, the first a little over and the last a little under 4,000 feet; Shrews-

Scene at Randolph.

VERMONT SCENES.

Roxbury.

Silent Cliff, Hancock.

A Hancock Pasture.

Granville.

Near the Connecticut.

bury Mountain, 4,086 feet, and Killington Peak, 3,924 feet, both in Rutland county; Equinox Mountain in Manchester, Bennington county, 3,706 feet, and Ascutney Mountain in Windsor, 3,320 feet. The surface of Vermont is generally uneven. A tract along Lake Champlain, widening in Addison county to 15 miles or more, is comparatively level; but with this exception the whole surface of the state consists of hills and valleys, alluvial flats and gentle acclivities, elevated plains and mountains. The hills are mostly yet crowned with timber, sugar orchards of maple covering the more accessible slopes, while the mountains still attest the name "Verd Mont" by bearing, nearly or quite to their summits, their growth of green, much of it being spruce, fir and hemlock that carry their dark green foliage throughout the year.

The rivers and streams of Vermont are very numerous, but for the most part small. They, in most cases, rise in the Green Mountains, and their courses are short and generally rapid. Connecticut River washes the whole eastern border of the state, and receives the waters of more than a third of its territory. Its Vermont tributaries are, besides numerous smaller streams, eleven rivers—the West, Saxton's, Williams', Black, Ottaquechee, White, Ompompanoosuc, Wait's, Wells, Passumpsic and Nulhegan. The Clyde, Barton and another Black River run northerly into Lake Memphremagog. Missisquoi, Lamoille, Winooski and Poultney Rivers and Otter Creek flow westerly into Lake Champlain, and the Battenkill and Hoosic westerly into Hudson River. Deerfield River runs southerly from Vermont and falls into the Connecticut in Massachusetts, and the Coaticook and Pike Rivers rise in the north part of the state and flow northerly into Canada.

Few countries in the world are better supplied with pure and wholesome water than is Vermont. Much the larger part of the farms in the state are well watered by springs or brooks, and but few, except on the islands, are not near some considerable mill-stream. Stagnant water is rarely found. The waters of the lakes and ponds are usually clear and transparent, and the streams and springs are bright, pure and lively. The waters of the lakes, ponds and streams are universally soft and in general free from foreign substances, and the same may be said of most of the springs, especially on the Green Mountains and in the parts east of the main range. Small lakes and ponds are found in all parts of Vermont, and about two-thirds of Lake Champlain, and one-third of Memphremagog are within her borders.

DISCOVERIES AND EARLY SETTLEMENTS.

The first discovery of America by Europeans that we have record of was by the Norwegians. Iceland, which lies in both hemispheres, although much nearer to Greenland in the western than to Norway or the north of Scotland, the nearest contiguous land in the eastern, was discovered by them in 860 and colonized in 874. Greenland they colonized 50 to 100 years later, after which Lief, the son of the founder of the Greenland colony, and Bjorn sailed to the south along the banks of North America, landing and spending a winter at some point which they called Vinland, and which is supposed to have been near Rhode Island. Here a colony was founded and existed a number of years, but eventually was given up. Danish history states that America was repeatedly visited by the Icelanders in the 11th, 12th and 13th centuries, and that they penetrated along the coast as far as the Carolinas, but made no permanent settlements, and even the knowledge of their explorations was nearly or entirely lost.

August 3, 1492, Columbus sailed from Spain on a voyage of discovery. Delaying a month in the Canaries to refit, he started thence on the 6th of September and on the 12th of October came in sight of one of the Bahama Islands, where he landed, and which he named San Salvador. After the discovery of several other of the West India Islands, including Cuba and Hayti, at the latter of which he settled a small colony, Columbus returned to Spain, arriving March 5, 1493. In September of the same year he started from Cadiz on a second voyage, with 17 ships and 1500 men. In this trip he discovered the Caribbee Islands, Jamaica and others and returned in 1496. In 1497 he set out on a third expedition and this time landed at Paria on the coast of South America. In 1502 he made still another voyage to America, but without especial results. He died at Valladolid in Spain, May 20, 1506.

Cuba was colonized by the Spaniards in 1511, and Panama, the oldest city now existing in America, was founded by them in 1518. The Spanish colonies in America, unlike those afterwards founded by the French and English, were prosperous from the start. The expedition under Cortez that conquered Mexico, 1519-21, was fitted out in Cuba and that of Pizarro that overran Peru, 1532-3, was sent from Panama. The other possessions of Spain in South and Central America were La Plata, New Grenada, Yucatan, Guatamala, Chili, and Venezuela. These included the larger part of South and

The Summit. Hancock and Middlebury Pass.

The Gen. Nash Place. New Haven River.

SCENES IN NORWAY.

Central America, excepting Brazil, that was claimed and colonized about 1500 by the Portugese.

Florida was discovered by Ponce de Leon in 1512, and afterwards visited in 1530 by De Soto, who perished on the banks of the Mississippi. St. Augustine was founded by the Spaniards in 1565. California, the beautiful, together with Arizona, New Mexico, Nevada, Utah and parts of Colorado and Wyoming, were annexed to Mexico by the Spaniards, but luckily all these last territories were rescued from Spanish semi-civilization by becoming a part of the United States, Florida in 1821, and California in 1846.

On the 20th of April, 1534, Jacques Cartier, acting under the government of France, sailed from the town of St. Malo, Brittany, for Newfoundland (discovered by John Cabot in 1497), whose banks had now for a number of years been noted for their fisheries. He passed through the straits of Belle Isle, came near the island of Anticosti, and, the season being late, went back to France. The next year he returned with three vessels, leaving St. Malo the 19th of May and arriving in August at a small bay opposite the island of Anticosti. He named this bay St. Lawrence, a name that was afterwards applied to the entire gulf and the river that flows into it. He now ascended the river then called Hochelaga, reaching the Saguenay September 1. Arriving at the river St. Charles, near the present city of Quebec, he left his two larger vessels. With the smallest, a galleon of 40 tons, and two open boats, carrying in all 50 sailors, he continued up the river St. Lawrence to the Indian town of Hochelaga a little west of Mount Royal (Montreal), where he arrived on the 2d day of October. Of this trip Thompson says in his history of Vermont: "This was doubtless the first voyage ever made by civilized man into the interior of North America and the first advance of a civilized people into the neighborhood of the territory of Vermont."

October 4th Cartier began his return and on the 11th reached the ships that he had left. Building a fort on the island of Orleans, he passed the winter, during which many of his men died from the scurvy. With the opening of navigation the next spring he returned to France, arriving at St. Malo the 16th of July.

The fisheries off the banks of Newfoundland were established by the Portugese in 1500 and continued year by year by the French, Spanish, Portugese and English. In 1578, it is said, there were 400 vessels engaged in this trade. These fishermen, too, carried on a trade with the Indians for furs. In the mean time several attempts

were made by the French to establish colonies in America, at Port
Royal, Nova Scotia, Tadousac at the mouth of the Saguenay, St.
Croix, near the coast of Maine, and elsewhere, but none succeeded
until that under Champlain in 1608.

In 1607 the first permanent English settlement in America was
established in Jamestown, Va. In 1614 Manhattan Island was settled by the Dutch, and about the same time Fort Orange was built
at Albany. In 1620 the Pilgrims landed at Plymouth Rock and in
1629 the colony of Massachusetts Bay was established. In 1623
Plymouth and Dover, New Hampshire, were settled, followed by settlements in Exeter and Hampden in 1638–9. Rhode Island was
colonized from Massachusetts in 1636, and Connecticut in 1634–6.

The first white man known to have visited Vermont was
Samuel de Champlain, whose name will long live upon the
beautiful lake whose bright waters afforded him his entrance
way. He was born in 1567 at the small seaport of Brouage
on the bay of Biscay. He was a captain in the royal navy, but had
fought for the king in Brittany. The war over, he visited the West
Indies, having obtained the command of a Spanish ship bound for
that country. In this trip, which occupied two years and a half, besides the principal parts of the West Indian Islands, he visited Vera
Cruz and the City of Mexico, and returned by way of Panama. In
1603 he made his first voyage up the St. Lawrence as far as Montreal,
and in 1604 joined an expedition to Nova Scotia, where he remained
for two winters, exploring in that time the coast of North America as
far as Cape Cod.

On the 13th day of April, 1608, Champlain, with men, arms and
stores for a colony, sailed from Honfleur in France, and in June landed at the Indian town of Quebec, where he determined to establish
his colony, perceiving the great natural advantages of this site for a
military post. To the courage, talent and perseverance of Champlain, more than to any other man, the establishment of the French
in Canada is due. He remained in command of the colony of
Quebec until he died there on Christmas day, 1635, at the age of
sixty-eight.

In June, 1609, Champlain, with two other Frenchmen, accompanied a party of Algonquin Indians up the St. Lawrence from Quebec to the Richelieu River, thence up this stream to the lake it came
from. This lake was called by the Indians *Caniadcri-Guarunte*—
"Door of the Country." Continuing southward, he came to another
lake lying southwest of and near Lake Champlain and called by the

CANADIAN SCENES.
Quebec from Levis.
Golf Links, Murray Bay.

CANADIAN SCENES.
Bay St. Paul, below Quebec.
Capes Eternity and Trinity, Saguenay River.

natives Lake Horicon. This he christened Lake St. Sacrament, now Lake George. Here they encountered a band of Iroquois, long hostile to the Algonquins, and a battle ensued. The Frenchmen carried firearms, the terror and deadly effect of which soon routed the Iroquois, who probably had never before encountered foes armed with such weapons. Returning, the victors visited the Vermont side of the lake at Chimney Point, in Addison, and it was here that Champlain named the lake after himself. This was doubtless the first visit of Europeans to the territory of Vermont. The party returned to Tadousac at the mouth of the Saguenay, whither Champlain accompanied them.

This, it will be noted, was the same year that Captain Henry Hudson, then in the employ of the Dutch East India Company, discovered and sailed into the mouth of the river to which he gave his name. It was before any permanent settlement had been made by Europeans within the territory of the United States of America, except at St. Augustine in Florida.

When the French first visited Canada it was inhabited by the Huron and Algonquin Indians, between whom and the Iroquois (or Five Nations, afterwards Six Nations), whose headquarters were near Schenectady, there was constant war. The territory of Vermont does not seem to have been permanently occupied by Indians, but was used as a battle ground by these hostile nations. "Thus," says Thompson in his Civil History of Vermont, "so early as the year 1609, was Lake Champlain and the western borders of the present territory of Vermont discovered and partially explored by the French; and although after this event, more than a century elapsed before this tract of country became the residence of any civilized inhabitants, it was during this period and long after, the theatre of war and a scene of Indian havoc and cruelty of the most appalling character. But these wars were wholly carried on by Canadian Indians and the French, whose settlements were rapidly extending up the St. Lawrence, on the one part, and by the confederated nations of the Iroquois on the other, previous to the year 1664. This year the Dutch settlement of New Netherlands was surrendered to the English and its name changed to New York; and from this period the country now called Vermont, and Lake Champlain, became the great thoroughfare of the French and English colonies and their Indian allies in their almost incessant wars with each other." This latter contest, probably in a large degree because of the atrocities perpetrated by the Indians on both sides, grew into an "irrepressible conflict," ending only with the downfall of the French power in America when Wolfe took Quebec in 1760. To all appearance peace had now settled permanently over this long-distracted region. Immediately the settlement of Vermont began in earnest.

The Indians who were with Champlain on his first expedition into Lake Champlain were of the great family of the Algonquins, a nation composed of many tribes, loosely connected and often warring with each other, but speaking dialects of the same tongue. Their homes were scattered through the country from Canada on the north to Virginia on the south; from the sea coast on the east to Wisconsin, Illinois and Indiana on the west. The nation which Champlain had attacked and of whose chiefs three had fallen by his hand was the Iroquois, or Five Nations. They were made up of the Mohawks, Oneidas, Onondagas, Cayugas and Senecas. Their country, like a great island in the midst of the Algonquins, extended through central New York from the Hudson to the Genesee.

"Among all the barbarous nations of the continent, the Iroquois of New York stand paramount. Elements which among other tribes were crude, confused and embryotic were among them systematized and concreted into an established polity. The Iroquois was the Indian of Indians. A thorough savage, yet a finished and developed savage, he is perhaps an example of the highest elevation which man can reach without emerging from his primitive condition of the hunter. A geographical position commanding on one hand the portal of the Great Lakes, and on the other the sources of the streams flowing both to the Atlantic and the Mississippi, gave the ambitious and aggressive confederates advantages which they perfectly understood, and by which they profited to the utmost. Patient and politic as they were ferocious, they were not only conquerors of their own race, but the powerful allies and the dreaded foes of the French and English colonies, flattered and caressed by both, yet too sagacious to give themselves without reserve to either."
—*Parkman.*

Champlain and his victorious band returned exulting to the mouth of the Richelieu, where they separated, part of the Indians seeking their distant homes on the Ottawa, while the rest followed Champlain to Quebec. On the first night of their return journey, the savages, against the vehement remonstrances of Champlain, put to death by torture one of their Iroquois prisoners.

"Thus did New France rush into collision with the redoubted warriors of the Five Nations. Here was the beginning, in some

.n Grand Isle County.

measure doubtless the cause, of a long suite of murderous conflicts, bearing havoc and flame to generations yet unborn. Champlain had invaded the tiger's den; and now, in smothered fury, the patient savage would lie biding his day of blood."—*Parkman.*

"The Mohawks never forgot that fatal 30th of July, 1609. The manes of the three chiefs who then fell at the fire of the Frenchman's arquebus were not appeased until rivers of blood had flowed beneath the tomahawk of the avenger. For every feather in the waving plumes of these chieftains a bloody scalp was counted—for every triumphant shout of the victorious Hurons and Algonquins, in after years, an answering shout was returned."—*Palmer's History of Lake Champlain.*

The history of Lake Champlain, as connected with Vermont, is not resumed until 1642. From that time forward until the gallant McDonough annihilated the British fleet in front of Plattsburg in 1814, this doorway of the nation was the scene of ever-recurring contest and slaughter. In the space of this work we can give only an outline sketch of this tragic and thrilling chapter in the history of Vermont.

In the thirty-two years following 1609 the Iroquois had made many incursions into Canada which were almost uniformly successful. "In their attacks no force was too strong for them to overcome; no hiding place too secret for them to discover. So great, at length, became the audacity of these savages that they suddenly fell upon a body of Algonquins, under the very guns of the fortress of Quebec, and massacred them without mercy."—*Palmer.*

They were accustomed to reach the French settlements of Canada by way of Lake Champlain and the Richelieu River. To stop these inroads the French in 1641 built two forts on that river, and in 1642 M. de La Motte, a French captain, built a fort on the island just south of the source of that river in Lake Champlain, called Isle La Motte. This fort was named St. Anne, and was the first erected on Lake Champlain or within the present territory of Vermont.

The first incursion of the French, through the lake, to retaliate upon the Iroquois, was in January, 1666, fifty-seven years after Champlain's expedition, and while M. de Tracy was governor of Canada. In the heart of winter M. de Courcelles with five hundred men on snow-shoes marched up the Richelieu River and Lake Champlain to attack the Mohawks, by whom they were drawn into ambush about two miles from Schenectady and severely handled.

Having seen enough of the Mohawks, and being succored and saved
from death by cold and starvation by the English and Dutch settlers
of that region, they hurried back to Lake Champlain and Canada,
pursued part of the way by the Mohawks, and losing quite a
number, some of whom met their death by freezing. The next June
(1666) a peace was agreed upon between Governor de Tracy and the
Iroquois, news of which reached Fort St. Anne, causing a relaxation
of vigilance on the part of the French garrison, who ventured to
hunt and fish in the neighborhood. "While a small party of French
officers and soldiers were thus engaged, they were suddenly attacked
by a band of Mohawk Indians, who killed Captains de Travesy and
de Chazy and took several volunteers prisoners. Information was
immediately sent to Quebec, and one of the Indian deputies had the
vain audacity to boast at M. de Tracy's table that he had slain the
officers with his own hand. The Indian was seized and strangled on
the spot; and M. de Tracy, breaking off all negotiations, sent M. de
Sorel, at the head of 300 men, against the Mohawk villagers, with
orders to overrun the whole country and to put every inhabitant to
the sword. M. de Sorel had, by forced marches, crossed Lake Champlain, and was pushing rapidly toward the Indian villages, when he
was met by a new deputation from the Mohawks, bringing back the
Frenchmen taken prisoners near Fort St. Anne, and offering every
satisfaction for the murders committed there. Still desirous to
secure peace, and in the belief that the demonstration already made
had over-awed the Indians, M. de Sorel retraced his steps to
Quebec, where negotiations were again resumed with such success
that on the 12th of July, 1666, a treaty was signed by which the
Indians agreed to return the Canadian, Algonquin and Huron prisoners in their hands, and to become the fast friends and allies of the
French. On the other part the viceroy promised to extend his pro-
tection over their nation, to send some Jesuit missionaries among
them and to open trade and commerce by Lake St. Sacrament (Lake
George)."—*Palmer.*

This peace seems to have lasted something over a month. In
September of the same year (1666) we find collected at Fort St. Anne
600 veteran French regulars, as many more French volunteers
(*habitans*) and 100 Algonquin and Huron warriors, all mustered
there by M. Talon, intendant of New France. Early in October
this formidable army, personally commanded by Governor de Tracy
(despite his advanced years), moved up the lake in 300 batteaux,
taking along two small pieces of cannon, and advanced into the

CANADIAN SCENES.
Dalhousie East.
Tadousac.

Scenes Near Bread Loaf Inn.

Mohawk country. The Mohawk warriors were appalled by the immense array and fled to the hills, leaving their villages, their strong palisades and their provisions in charge of women and a few old men too feeble to escape, and who were taken prisoners. De Tracy burned all the villages, destroyed all the provisions that he could not carry away, and returned by way of Lake Champlan, his only recorded losses being that of eight persons drowned in the lake by the capsizing of two canoes in a storm. This experience effectually quieted the Mohawks for the next twenty years. Their villages thus destroyed were in the vicinity of Schenectady.

The accession of William and Mary in 1689 was followed by a war between the English and the French which lasted eight years. The spirit of the combat was soon communicated to the colonists in America. As a result, it was resolved by the French in Canada that an army of French and Indians should pass up Lake Champlain and attack Albany and the other English settlements in that vicinity. It was also planned that a French fleet should at the same time attack the city of New York, the ultimate design being to break completely the power of the English in the colony of New York and subdue their inveterate enemy, the Iroquois, now augmented by the Tuscaroras and called the Six Nations.

These fierce warrors had indeed shown themselves worthy of attention. The forts of St. Anne and of St. Theresa (the upper fort on the Richelieu) had gone to decay and Montreal was defended only by rotting palisades. The only work of any strength left was the lower fort on the Richelieu at Chambly, which had been rebuilt of stone, and was surrounded by a settlement. On the 12th of November, 1687, the Iroquois fell upon this fort in great force, but were unsuccessful, through they ravaged the settlement. "A few days later the whole country between the St. Lawrence and the Richelieu swarmed with a savage host, who demanded immediate audience with the governor, M. de Denonville, and haughtily dictated peace to the weak and terrified inhabitants. 'Look', cried the proud chief, pointing toward a band of 1200 warriors at his back, 'we are like the leaves of the forest in number and stronger than the mighty oak. Your people are few and weak. We have no occasion to lift our whole hand, for our little finger is sufficient to destroy you.' Denonville bowed before a storm he could not resist and concluded a treaty of peace on the terms proposed by the savages."—*Palmer*.

This peace was short lived. The next July (1688) the Iroquois again burst into Canada, burned Montreal, and broke up most of the frontier settlements.

These calamities had so crippled the colony that Frontenac, viceroy of Canada in 1689, found himself unable to make the projected descent upon the New York colony. He did, however, the following winter, send out two parties, one of which destroyed the fort at Salmon Falls, N. H., slaying 30 English and taking 54 prisoners. The other party, commanded by D'Aillebout, and consisting of 200 French and 50 Indians, left Montreal for Schenectady by way of Lake Champlain early in January, 1690. They were so pinched by hunger and cold on arriving near Schenectady that they seriously thought of giving themselves up to the English as prisoners; but learning from their spies that Schenectady was in no condition for defence, in the darkness of night they entered the village, which they completely sacked and burned, killing 60 and taking away 27 prisoners and 40 horses. Those of the villagers who escaped the enemy fled through the snow to Albany, 14 miles distant; but many were nearly naked and no less than 25 who reached Albany lost limbs by freezing.

The next May (1690) the English colonies resolved to proceed against Quebec from the east by water, and to attack Montreal at the same time by proceeding through Lake Champlain with a combined force of whites and Iroquois Indians. The fleet was not got ready until too late in the season, and the Iroquois refused to join the settlers, so this entire enterprise was abandoned. But Capt. John Schuyler of Albany, with a band of 29 white volunteers and 120 Indians, made an expedition in canoes in August, 1690, down Lake Champlain and the Richelieu, to a point one mile above Chambly, whence he marched to La Prairie, on the south shore of the St. Lawrence, about 15 miles distant. This settlement they burned, killing six and taking 19 prisoners. They also destroyed many cattle, but retired without attacking the fort. The next June (1691) Major Philip Schuyler left Albany with 150 English and 300 Indians, and taking the same route that his brother John had taken the summer before, surprised and captured the fort at La Prairie. De Callieres, then governor of Montreal, crossed the St. Lawrence with 800 troops, when Schuyler retreated to the woods and destroyed a small detachment sent to cut off his retreat. Thereupon M. de Callieres came up with a large force and a desperate battle of an hour and a half ensued. Schuyler's men were posted behind trees, and his loss was trifling, while the enemy, more exposed, lost about 200 in killed and wounded. Schuyler safely drew off his men and returned to Albany. These favorable results gave new impetus to the warlike spirit of the Iro-

Montreal from Mt. Royal.

La Canadienne.

quois, who so harassed the French for the next two years that Frontenac determined again to invade their territory. Braving the ter-
rors of another winter march, he set out from Montreal in January,
1693, with 600 French and Indians, by the old Champlain route for
the Mohawk valley, where he surprised the first Mohawk village,
slew many of the inhabitants, took more than 300 prisoners and
returned. He was pursued by Major Schuyler with a force of
about 300, who succeeded in recapturing about fifty of the
prisoners.

These reciprocal depredations ceased with the treaty of peace
between England and France in 1697. But in 1702 war broke out
again in Europe and was as usual communicated to the colonies.
In the winter of 1704 a party of 300 French and Indians moved up
Lake Champlain to the Winooski River, followed up that river and
down the White and Connecticut Rivers to the flourishing settlement of
Deerfield, Mass., which they reached on the 29th of February. This
village they surprised and overpowered, at the dead of night, slew
47 of the citizens, captured the rest, burned the town, and returned
to Canada with their prisoners and booty.

For several years after the destruction of Deerfield, the
frontiers, both of the New England provinces and Canada, were the
scenes of frequent massacre and devastation. In 1709 and 1711
formidable preparations for the invasion of Canada by the colonists,
on the plan of 1690, that is, by attacking Quebec with a fleet to
come up the St. Lawrence, and Montreal at the same by an army
coming through Lake Champlain, were frustrated. In 1709 a force
of 2,000 men was gathered at Fort Anne on Wood Creek, near the
southern extremity of Lake Champlain; but the fleet which was to
co-operate was ordered elswhere, and the expedition was abandoned.
In 1711, an army of 4000 men marched from Albany to Lake
George, while another army of 6400 men sailed from Boston on 68
transports for a simultaneous attack on Quebec. But the British
admiral approached too near a small island in the narrow and
dangerous chanel of Traverse, when a sudden squall scattered the
fleet, and drove eight vessels on the rocks, where they were wrecked
and a multitude of men, variously estimated at from 1000 to 3000,
were drowned. Thereupon the expedition was abandoned and the
army at Lake George was marched back to Albany and disbanded.
Thus terminated the third attempt of the English to conquer Canada.
Some relief was gained, however, by the treaty of Utrecht, concluded
in 1713, by which France released its nominal sovereignty over the

Iroquois, and recognized the dominion of Great Britian over their territory.

"As yet no settlements had been permanently established in the valley of Lake Champlain. Fort St. Anne, built in 1665, had been occupied for a few years and then abandoned. Fort Anne, erected by Col. Nicholson on Wood Creek in 1709, was burned by him on the return of his army to Albany in 1711. In 1713, Fort Saratoga was the nearest post to the lake on the south, and Forts La Prairie and Chambly on the north. No settlements were commenced within the present limits of Vermont until after the erection of Fort Dummer on the Connecticut River in 1724."—*Palmer.*

In this statement Mr. Palmer and some other historians are mistaken. It is entirely certain that in April, 1690, Capt. Jacobus De Warm, under the authority of New York, crossed with a small party from Crown Point to Chimney Point in Addison, and there built "the little stone fort," long after used by the provincials and English. This was the first occupation of Vermont soil by civilized men. *what about said St. Anne - 1665 ?*

Fort St. Frederic was built by the French at Crown Point, N. Y., (opposite Chimney Point, Vt.) in 1731, and enlarged and strengthened in 1734. The English claimed title to both sides of the lake and remonstrated strongly, but took no steps to prevent this fortification of the narrow lake by the French. Soon after this fort was built a considerable settlement was formed about it on both sides of the lake, "composed principally of the families of old soldiers who had been paid off and discharged from service. The houses of some of the settlers were convenient and comfortable, but the majority lived in mere cabins built of boards. Until 1759 St. Frederic was the seat of the French power on the lake. Here was the rallying point for the fierce Abenaquis from the St. Francis, the Arundacks of the fertile Ottawa, and the warlike Wyandots of the West—drawn together by a common love of revenge or the hope of plunder. Here the ferocious Outagamis, the restless Algonquin and the vindictive Huron met to recount their deeds of horrid barbarity. At one moment would be heard the vesper bell of the little chapel calling the rude but virtuous husbandman, the scarred veteran of France, and the voluble Canadian to their evening prayers; while at the next the rocky shore would echo to the loud whoop of the merciless savage, returning from some successful attack upon the neighboring settlements. Long had the English colonists cause to regret the want of vigilance and forecast on the part of their rulers,

Contre-Cœur, Province of Quebec, Canada.

Ice Palace, Montreal.

Toboggan Slides, Montreal.

which permitted the French to seize and retain this controlling position on the lake."—*Palmer*.

The settlements about Fort St. Frederic extended to Chimney Point and adjacent parts of Addison on the Vermont shore and are estimated to have numbered as many as 600 souls on both sides of the lake. This fort, in 1742, was considered the strongest work held by the French on this continent save Quebec.

From the year 1725 a long peace ensued between France and England, and between the colonies as well. But in 1744 Great Britian and France were again at war, and the English now perceived their extreme folly in permitting the French to establish themselves at Crown Point. The extreme northern post held by the English in western New England was Hoosic Fort at Williamstown, Mass., near the southwest corner of Vermont. This was captured by French and Indians from Crown Point in August, 1746. There were several small forts near Fort Dummer on the west side of the Connecticut. One of these, Bridgman's Fort in Vernon, was also taken by the French in 1747. In April of that year the French and Indians besieged the fort at Number 4, now Charlestown, N. H., the most northerly English post on that river; but it was bravely and successfully defended by Capt. Phineas Stevens with 30 men. The war lasted till 1749 and the frontiers were continually harassed, but no other considerable expedition was undertaken on either side.

Frontier depredations continued till 1755, when a combined effort on the part of the English colonies was determined upon. The English had then practically no defensive works on their frontier, while the French had fortifications at Duquesne, Niagara, Crown Point and Beau-Sejour. It was determined that an expedition should be sent against each of these forts. That against Duquesne, under Gen. Braddock, resulted in an ambuscade and the frightful calamity known as Braddock's Defeat. That against Niagara effected nothing; that against Beau-Sejour was never sent, while the expedition against Fort St. Frederic resulted in much severe fighting, with severe losses on both sides, the advantage being with the English, but failed of its object by reason, as it would seem, of the inefficiency of Gen. Johnson, who commanded the English forces. These campaigns are made more conspicious by the facts that Col. George Washington with his Virginians saved Braddock's army from total destruction, while Capt. Israel Putnam distinguished himself in the army of Gen. Johnson.

In 1756 little was done by either party in the vicinity of Lake Champlain. The English completed Fort William Henry on Lake

George, while the French fortified Ticonderoga. In March, 1757, Fort William Henry was attacked by a force of 1500 French and Indians, who were repulsed by an inferior force under John Stark, twenty years later the hero of Bennington. Gen. Montcalm assumed command of the French, and by the cowardice of Gen. Webb was enabled to capture Fort William Henry after a siege of six days, during which it was gallantly defended by Col. Monro. Montcalm agreed in the terms of surrender that Monro's forces might march out with their baggage to Fort Edward, only a few miles distant; but he was unable to restrain his Indians, who fell upon the retreating column and slew large numbers, including women and children, keeping up the massacre half way to Fort Edward, when the living were rescued by a detachment from that fort, where Webb had all this time lain with an army of 4000 inactive men, declining to come to the rescue. Fort William Henry was razed to the ground. The French returned to Ticonderoga, and resumed work upon Fort Carillon, a formidable fortress which they erected at the point between the outlet of Lake George and Lake Champlain, near the present ruins of the later Fort Ticonderoga.

The next year (1758), the British had by July 1 a noble army of over 15,000 at the head of Lake George around the ruins of Fort William Henry. Well furnished with artillery and supplies, this proud host on July 4th moved down the waters of Lake George in more than a thousand boats to take Fort Carillon, defended by Montcalm with about 3600 men. But that intrepid leader, whose courage seemed to be fired by the enormous odds, fortified across the narrow neck west of Fort Carillon and between the swamp and the outlet to Lake George, and felled trees and made an almost impassible abbatis in front of his works. On this narrow ground only a small part of Abercrombie's great force could operate at once, which could be opposed by an equal number fighting under cover. With singular fatuity Abercrombie, without using his artillery, which would speedily have demolished the works, pushed his infantry against them. "As the columns approached, and when the ranks became entangled among the logs and fallen trees which protected the breastwork, Montcalm opened a galling fire of artillery and musketry, which mowed down the brave officers and men by hundreds, For four hours the English vainly strove to cut their way through the impenetrable abbatis, until Abercrombie, despairing of success, and having already lost 1944 men in killed and wounded, ordered a retreat. Montcalm did not pursue, for the English still

Canada—Primitive and Modern.

outnumbered him four-fold. Having refreshed his exhausted soldiers, he employed the night in strengthening his lines—a useless
labor, for the frightened Abercrombie did not stop until he reached
the head of Lake George, and even then he sent his artillery and
ammunition to Albany for safety."—*Palmer*. Among the English
killed was young Lord Howe, called the idol of the army. He fell
by the side of Israel Putnam while making a reconnoisance in force
at the beginning of the battle.

A few days later, Major Israel Putnam, who was scouting for the
English, met one of those terrible adventures which marked his
career. He was captured by Indians of Marin's command, who
bound him to a tree, where a young savage amused himself by
throwing his tomahawk and sticking it in the tree as near as he
could to the prisoner's head without hitting it. A Canadian came
up, snapped his fusee at Putnam's breast, prodded him in the ribs
with the muzzle and banged him on the jaw with the butt of the gun.
The Indians then stripped him, bound him to a tree, piled dry
bushes about him and set them on fire. But before the torture was
begun, Marin, the commander, appeared, scattered the fire and released the victim, whom he delivered, little the worse for his frightful experience, to Montcalm, by whom he was sent to Montreal.

Thus had three great efforts of the English to regain possession
of Lake Champlain failed. "Johnson was inefficient, Webb pusillan-
imous and Abercrombie wanting in military skill and firmness. The
first halted his army to build a fort [William Henry] when he should
have captured one [Crown Point]; the second with 4000 men
under his immediate command abandoned the brave Monro to the
tomahawk; while Abercrombie, though far superior to both, by a
false move and 'the extremest fright and consternation', allowed less
than 4000 men to repel the advance of 15,000 troops, truly said to
have been the largest and best appointed army in America. Success, however, had attended the British arms in other quarters.
Louisburg capitulated to Gen. Amherst in July, and in November
Gen. Forbes was in possession of Fort Duquesne."—*Palmer*.

But the beginning of the end was now at hand. In 1759 Gen.
Amherst, commander-in-chief of the British forces in America, a
daring and accomplished soldier, took personal command in this
region. When he came down Lake George, in June, and cautiously
proceeded to invest Fort Carillon, De Bourlemaque, the French commander, blew up and abandoned that fortress. He retreated to
Crown Point, where he also dismantled the fort, burned the settle-

ments and retreated to Isle Aux Noix. The glory of St. Frederic was departed. Crown Point was once more in the hands of the English. Amherst, who reached Crown Point in August with his army, immediately set about building a new fort about 200 yards west of the old Fort St. Frederic. "This fort, although never completed, is said to have cost the English government over two millions of pounds sterling. The ramparts were about twenty-five feet thick and nearly the same in height and were built of solid masonry. The curtains varied in length from 52 to 100 yards, and the whole circuit, measuring around the ramparts and including the bastions, was 853 yards. A broad ditch surrounded the work. On the north was a gate, and from the northeast bastion a covered way leading to the water."—*Palmer*.

Gen. Amherst also, with the greatest dispatch, caused three armed vessels to be built, which were completed by the 11th of October. With these he destroyed the French fleet, a schooner and three sloops, at Valcour Island. After making two attempts to move his army in batteaux to Canada, he returned, baffled by the winds, to winter quarters at Crown Point on the 21st of October.

While Amherst was at Crown Point he opened a road from that place to Number Four on the Connecticut river (Charlestown, N. H.). He also sent Major Rogers, of the New Hampshire troops, to destroy the village of the St. Francis Indians on the south side of the St. Lawrence near Three Rivers. These Indians were noted for their atrocious cruelties to the English. Rogers left his boats in Missisquoi Bay, where they were presently discovered and taken by the French.

He struck the Indian village by surprise on the night of October 4th, when his band, infuriated by the sight of several hundred English scalps hung up on poles, adopted the merciless tactics of the savages themselves, spared neither age nor sex, slew more than two-thirds of the three hundred villagers, destroyed the town utterly by fire and turned back with twenty prisoners and five English captives whom he had retaken. He directed his course toward Coos on the Connecticut. Being pursued, he led the enemy into an ambuscade and turned them back with great loss. He reached the Connecticut River at the mouth of the Passumpsic, where he had arranged to have provisions sent, but found none. He here disbanded his followers all in starving condition and made his way to Charlestown, where most of his band after terrible sufferings arrived, and were led back by Rogers over the new road to Amherst's army at Crown Point. In

Bridge over Connecticut, near Brattleboro.

Valley Fair Coaching Parade, Brattleboro.

the attack on the village, only one of the English was killed, but on this long and terrible return route 49 men were lost.

In the meantime General Wolfe had scaled the heights above Quebec, conquered and slain Montcalm on the Plains of Abraham, and lost his own life in the same battle; and on the 18th of September, 1759, the great fortress of Quebec, so long the seat of the French power in America, was surrendered to Wolfe's victorious army. Gen. Amherst with Crown Point as a basis of operations annoyed the enemy by various incursions during the early summer of 1760. In August he sent Col. Haviland with something over 3000 troops against the French at Isle Aux Noix (near Rouses Point) their final stronghold in Lake Champlain. Haviland encamped opposite this French post and bombarded it for three days, when the garrison surrendered on the 27th of August. On the 8th of September, Haviland joined Amherst and Murray under the walls of Montreal, and on the same day that city was surrendered by Vaudreuil. By this act, the French dominion in Canada ceased, and by the treaty of peace signed in Paris on the 10th of February, 1763, that Province was formally ceded to Great Britain. Thus was completed a conquest then deemed the most important that the British arms had ever achieved.

THE DOVES AT MENDON.

(BY MRS. JULIA C. R. DORR.)

"Coo ! coo ! coo !" says Arné,
Calling the doves at Mendon !

Under the vine-clad porch she stands,
A gentle maiden with willing hands,
Dropping the grains of yellow corn.
Low and soft, like a mellow horn,
While the sunshine over her fall,
Over and over she calls and calls
   "Coo ! coo ! coo !" to the doves—
   The happy doves at Mendon.

   "Coo ! coo ! coo" says Arné,
   Calling the doves at Mendon !

Down they flutter with timid grace,
Lured by the voice and the tender face,
Till the evening air is all astir
With the happy strife and the eager whir.
One by one, and two by two,
And then a rush through the ether blue;
   While Arné scatters the yellow corn
   For the gentle doves at Mendon.

   "Coo ! coo ! coo !" says Arné,
   Calling the doves at Mendon !

They hop on the porch where the baby sits,
They come and go as a shadow flits,
Now here, now there, while in and out
They crowd and jostle each other about;
Till one, grown bolder than all the rest—
A snow-white dove with an arching breast—
   Softly lights on her outstretched hand
   Under the vines at Mendon.

   "Coo ! coo ! coo !" says Arné,
   Calling the doves at Mendon !

With a rush and a whir of shining wings,
They hear and obey—the dainty things !

Mrs. Julia C. R. Dorr.

"The Doves at Mendon."

Dun and purple and snowy white,
Clouded gray, like the soft twilight,
Straight as an arrow shot from a bow,
Wheeling and circling high and low,
    Down they fly from the slanting roof
    Of the old red barn at Mendon.

    "Coo! coo! coo!" says Arné,
    Calling the doves at Mendon!

Baby Alice with wide blue eyes
Watches them ever with new surprise,
While she and Wag on the mat together
Joy in the soft midsummer weather.
Hither and thither she sees them fly,
Gray and white on the azure sky,
    Light and shadow against the green
    Of the maple grove at Mendon.

    "Coo! coo! coo!" says Arné,
    Calling the doves at Mendon!

A sound, a motion, a flash of wings—
They are gone—like a dream of heavenly things.
The doves are flown and the porch is still,
And the shadows gather on vale and hill.
Then sinks the sun, and the mountain breeze
Stirs the tremulous maple-trees;
    While Love and Peace, as the night comes down,
    Brood over quiet Mendon!

CHAPTER II.

PIONEER SETTLEMENTS.   STRUGGLE WITH NEW YORK.

ONE effect of the English conquest was to change the territory of Vermont from a battle ground to a land eagerly sought by settlers. The provincial troops had traversed much of its area, had passed over the road opened by Amherst from Lake Champlain to the Connecticut, and had thus become acquainted with the fertility of the soil, and the desirability of the country for rural homes. The country was so ripe for settlement that its population, not over 300 in 1760 and not greatly increased until the treaty of Paris in 1763, was about 7,000 in 1770, 20,000 in 1775, 30,000 in 1780, 85,000 in 1791 and over 154,000 in 1800, within the present limits of Vermont. This influx of population amazed Burgoyne, who in a letter to Lord Germain, dated Saratoga, Aug. 20, 1777, says: "The Hampshire grants in particular, a country unpeopled and almost unknown in the last war, now abounds in the most active and most rebellious race on the continent, and hangs like a gathering storm on my left."

"When the French army retreated to Canada, it was accompanied by the few inhabitants residing upon the borders of the lake. There was, however, at this time, a settlement of French and Indians at Swanton Falls in Vermont, several miles east of the lake, containing a small church, a saw-mill and about fifty huts, which was not abandoned by them until the year 1775. . . .

"In 1776, Colonel Ephraim Doolittle, Paul Moore, Marshall Newton and others settled in the town of Shoreham, and in the same year Donald McIntosh, a native of Scotland, moved into the town of Vergennes. A saw mill was erected at the lower falls of Otter Creek as early as 1769, and shortly afterwards a grist-mill was built at same place (Vergennes).

"John Strong, Zadock Everest and a Mr. Ward commenced a settlement in the town of Addison, on the opposite side of the lake from Crown Point, in 1769 or 1770. A settlement was also commenced in 1770, in the town of Panton, by John Pangborn and Odle

At Bread Loaf.   On the Road.

At Middlebury.

Road up the Mountain.

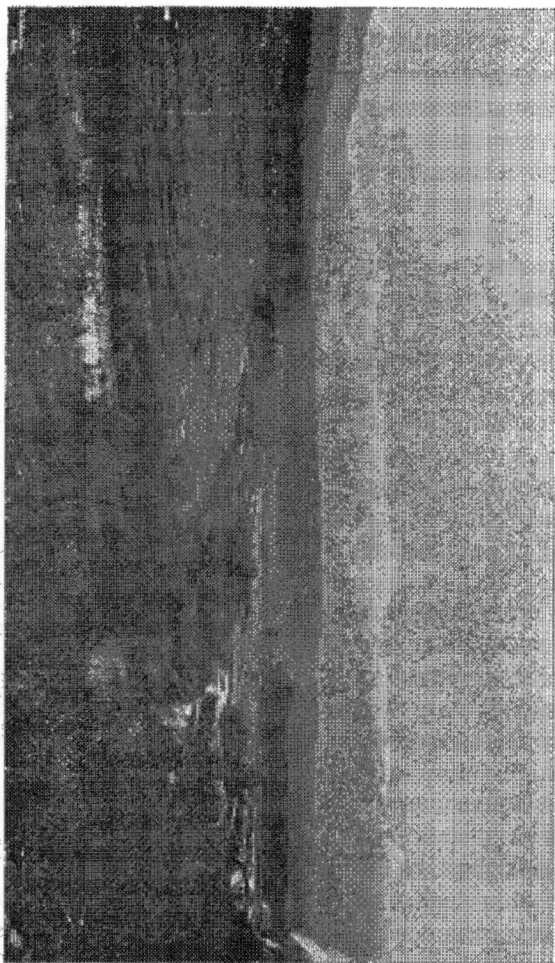

White Mountains.

Squires, who were afterwards joined by Timothy Spaulding, Peter Ferris and others. Ferris resided at the bay in which Arnold burned his vessels during the Revolutionary War.

"The town of Bridport was first settled, in 1768, by Philip Stone, of Groton, Massachusetts. About the same time, two families by the name of Richardson and Smith moved into the township and commenced a settlement, under New York titles, and were followed by Towner, Chipman and Plumer who held grants from the Governor of New Hampshire. In 1773, Samuel Smith moved his family into the town and was followed during the next winter by Mr. Victory. A settlement was commenced at the lower falls on the Winooski River by Ira Allen and Remember Baker, in 1773."—*Palmer*.

"When the English commenced their establishment at Fort Dummer (1724) that fort was supposed to lie within the limits of Massachusetts, and the settlements in that vicinity were first made under grants from that provincial government. But after a long and tedious controversy between Massachusetts and New Hampshire respecting their division line, King George II. finally decreed, on the 5th of March, 1740, that the northern boundry of the province of Massachusetts be 'a similar curve line, pursuing the course of the Merimac river, at three miles distant on the north side thereof, beginning at the Atlantic Ocean, and ending at a point due north of Pawtucket Falls; and a straight line drawn from thence due west until it meets his majesty's other governments.'

"This line was surveyed by Richard Hazen, in 1741, when Fort Dummer (now Brattleboro) was found to lie beyond the limits of Massachusetts to the north; and as the king of Great Britain repeatedly recommended to the assembly of New Hampshire to make provision for its support, it was generally supposed to have fallen within the jurisdiction of that province; and being situated on the west side of the Connecticut, it was supposed that New Hampshire extended as far westward as Massachusetts; that is, to a line twenty miles east of Hudson River.

" In the year 1741, Benning Wentworth was commissioned governor of the province of New Hampshire. On the 3d of January, 1749, he made a grant of a township of land six miles square, situated, as he conceived, on the western border of New Hampshire, being twenty miles east of the Hudson, and six miles north of Massachusetts line This township, in allusion to his own name, he called Bennington. About the same time, a correspondence was opened between him and the governor of the province of New York, in which were urged their respective titles to the lands on the west side of Connecticut River, yet without regard to these interfering claims, Wentworth proceeded to make further grants.

"These grants had amounted to 15 townships in 1754, but, this year, hostilities were commenced between the French and English colonies, which put a stop to further applications and grants till the close of the war, in 1760. * * *

"The governor of New Hampshire, by advice of his council, now ordered a survey to be made of Connecticut River for sixty miles, and three tiers of townships to be laid out on each side. As the applications for lands still increased, further surveys were ordered to be made, and so numerous were the applications that during the year 1761 no less than sixty townships of six miles square were granted on the west side of Connecticut River. The whole number of grants, in one or two years more, had amounted to one hundred and thirty-eight. Their extent was from Connecticut River on the east to what was esteemed twenty miles east of Hudson River, so far as that river extended to the northward, and after that as far westward as Lake Champlain." These lands were known as the New Hampshire Grants.

"By the fees and other emoluments, which Wentworth received in return for these grants, and by reserving five hundred acres in each township for himself, he was evidently accumulating a large fortune. The government of New York, wishing to have the profits of these lands, became alarmed at the proceedings of the governor of New Hampshire, and determined to check them. For this purpose Cadawallader Colden, lieutenant-governor of New York, on the 28th of December, 1763, issued a proclamation, in which he recited the grants made by Charles II. to the Duke of York, in 1664, and in 1674, which (as he claimed) embraced among other parts all the lands from the west side of Connecticut River to the east side of Delaware Bay. Founding his claim upon this grant, he ordered the sheriff of the county of Albany to make returns of the names of all persons who had taken possession of lands on the west side of the Connecticut, under titles derived from the government of New Hampshire.

"To prevent the effects which this proclamation was calculated to produce, and to inspire confidence in the validity of the New Hampshire grants, the governor of New Hampshire, on his part, put forth a counter proclamation, on the 13th of March, 1764, in which he declared that the grant to the Duke of York was obsolete,—that New Hampshire extended as far west as Massachusetts and Connec-

Brimfield, Massachusetts.

Lancaster, New Hampshire.

licut, and that the grants made by New Hampshire would be confirmed by the crown if the jurisdiction should be altered. He exhorted the settlers to be industrious and diligent in cultivating their lands, and not to be intimidated by the threatenings of New York. He required all the civil officers to exercise jurisdiction as far west as grants had been made, and to punish all disturbers of the peace. This proclamation served to quiet the minds of the settlers. Having purchased their lands under a charter from a royal governor, and after such assurances from him, they had no idea that a controversy between the two provinces, respecting the extent of their jurisdiction, would ever affect the validity of their titles."—*Thompson's Vermont.*

New York had hitherto founded her claim to the lands in question upon the grant to the Duke of York, but choosing no longer to rely on so precarious a tenure, application was now made to the crown for a confirmation of the claim. The application was supported by a petition, *purporting* to be signed by a great number of the settlers on the New Hampshire grants, representing that it would be for their advantage to be annexed to the colony of New York, and praying that the western bank of Connecticut River might be established as the eastern boundary of that province. In consequence of this petition and application of the government of New York the king in council on the 20th of July, 1764, did "order and declare the western banks of the river Connecticut, from where it enters the province of Massachusetts Bay, as far north as the 45th degree of northern latitude, to be the boundary line between the said two provinces of New Hampshire and New York." This determination does not appear to be founded on any previous grant, but was a decision which the wishes and convenience of the people were erroneously supposed to demand.

"Surprised as were the settlers on the New Hampshire grants at this order, it produced in them no serious alarm. They regarded it as merely extending the jurisdiction of New York, in future, over their territory. To this jurisdiction they were willing to submit; but they had no apprehension that it could, in any way, affect their title to the lands upon which they had settled. Having purchased and paid for them, and obtained deeds of the same under grants from the crown, they could not imagine by what pervision of justice they could be compelled, by the same authority, to re-purchase their lands or abandon them. The governor of New Hampshire, at first, remonstrated against this change of jurisdiction; but was, at length, induced to abandon the contest, and issued a proclamation recommending to the

proprietors and settlers due obedience to the authority and laws of
the colony of New York.

"The royal decree by which the division line between New
Hampshire and New York was established, was regarded very differ-
ently by the different parties concerned. The settlers on the New
Hampshire grants considered that it only placed them *thereafter*
under the jurisdiction of New York, and to this they were willing to
submit; but they had no idea that their titles to their lands, or that
any past transactions, could be affected by it. Had the government
of New York given the royal decision the same interpretation, no controversy would ever have arisen. The settlers would have acknowledged its jurisdiction and submitted to its authority without a murmur.
But that government gave the decision a very different construction.
It contended that the order had a *retrospective* operation, and decided
not only what should thereafter be, but what had always been, the
eastern limit of New York, and consequently, that the grants made
by New Hampshire were illegal and void.

"With these views, the government of New York proceeded to
extend its jurisdiction over the New Hampshire grants. The settlers
were called upon to surrender their charters, and re-purchase their
lands under grants from New York. Some of them complied with
this order, but most of them peremptorily refused. The lands of
those who did not comply were therefore granted to others, in whose
names actions of ejectment were commenced in the courts at Albany,
and judgments invariably obtained against the settlers and original
proprietors.

"The settlers soon found that they had nothing to hope from the
customary forms of law, and therefore determined upon resistance to
the unjust and arbitrary decisions of the court, till his Majesty's pleasure should be further known. Having fairly purchased their lands of
one royal governor, they were determined not willingly to submit and
repurchase them, at an exorbitant price, of another; and when the
executive officers of New York came to eject the inhabitants from
their possessions, they met with avowed opposition, and were not
suffered to proceed in the execution of their business."—*Thompson's Vermont.*

As early as 1763, the colony of New York had granted land on
the lake to eighty-one or more reduced officers who had served in
the French and Indian wars; nearly one half of which was on the
east side of the lake, and covering parts of fourteen lake townships
chartered by the thrifty but retiring Gov. Wentworth of New Hamp-

Landslide at Fayston.

shire. New York also appropriated a large tract lying between Otter Creek and Mallet's Bay, for the disbanded soldiers of the recent wars. Charlotte County, extending on the north from Lake Memphremagog to the St. Regis River, and stretching south on both sides of the lake beyond its southern extremity, with county seat at Skenesborough (now Whitehall) was organized by New York about the same time. Thus jurisdictions clashed and new and unsettled lands were claimed by rival grantees.

The New York assembly by an act passed July 3, 1766, erected the county of Cumberland. This act was annulled the following year by the king, but was repassed by New York Feb. 20, 1768, and the county was chartered March 17 of that year. The charter limits were as follows: "Beginning in Massachusetts north line on the west bank of Connecticut River and running W. 10° N. about 26 miles to the southeast corner of Stamford; thence N. 13° E. 56 miles to the southeast corner of Socialborough, thence N. 53° E. 30 miles to the south corner of Tunbridge; thence along the south line of Tunbrige, Strafford and Thetford to Connecticut River, and down said river to the place of beginning." The county seat was first at Chester and afterwards at Westminster. After the organization of the state government Cumberland county retained that name till 1779, when it was changed to Windham. Socialborough was a township granted by New York comprising the territory of Rutland and Pittsford. Durham was what is now Clarendon.

As a specimen of the highhanded manner in which the rights of the settlers were attempted to be wrested from them, the following extract from an article on Bennington by N. B. Hall, in the Vermont Gazetteer, may be cited:

"Becoming thus alarmed for the security of their property, the settlers of the several towns in this part of the territory, which had been annexed to New York, appointed agents to apply to the governor of the province to protect them in their possessions. These agents, Samuel Robinson of Bennington and Jeremiah French of Manchester, accordingly repaired to New York city for that purpose, in the month of December, 1765. But, on making known their errand to the governor, they found the city speculators had been altogether too fast for them; that the largest and most valuable portions of their land had been already granted; and that, for the poorer land that remained, the enormous patent fees which were demanded, would be fully equivalent to the actual value of the soil.

"Among the lands which had thus been granted, there may be

mentioned as characteristic of the others, a grant of 26,000 acres by
the name of Princetown, to John Taber Kempe, James Duane and
Walter Rutherford, being a tract some twelve miles in length, by
about four in breadth, and embracing the whole of the rich valley of
the Battenkill, which is included in the townships of Manchester and
Sunderland, and the largest part of that in Arlington; and a grant of
10,000 acres to Crean Brush, covering considerable portions of the
southwesterly part of Bennington and the northwesterly part of Pow-
nal. The persons who have been named, for whose benefit these
grants were made, were the three leading New York city land grab-
bers—Kempe, the first named, being attorney general of the province,
Duane the lawyer who led in prosecuting the claims under the York
patents, and Rutherford a merchant speculator. It was well known
in New York that these lands had long been granted by the province
of New Hampshire, and were actually occupied under such grants,
and the patents were procured in utter disregard of the rights and
claims of the settlers."

Representatives from the several towns met in the fall of 1766,
and appointed Samuel Robinson of Bennington their agent to the
king to represent the grievances of the settlers and obtain, if possible,
a confirmation of the New Hampshire grants. By force of his repre-
sentations the royal order of June, 1767, annulling the New York act
which created the county of Cumberland, was issued; and on the 24th
of July following the governor of New York was prohibited by special
order of the king in council from making "any further grants whatso-
ever of the lands in question, till his majesty's further pleasure should
be known concerning the same." Most unfortunately Samuel Robinson died in London the next October, leaving his work unfinished.

The manner of obtaining these grants was very simple. If one
wanted a tract of 10,000 to 100,000 acres, he had only to locate it by
general bounds in such fertile region as he might choose, then apply
to the governor in the name of himself and such number of associates
as the size of the tract demanded at 1000 acres each, representing
that they intended to settle on such tract, or to people the same with
their tenants; when the same would be granted to the whole company
as tenants in common. Thereupon, all the associates would quit
claim their rights to the leading land thief, and his title was complete.
It was in this way that John Taber Kempe, James Duane, Walter
Rutherford, and a few other favorites of the royal governors obtained
grants amounting to more than 2,000,000 acres of the choicest parts
of Vermont. Of course the governors did not act for nothing, but

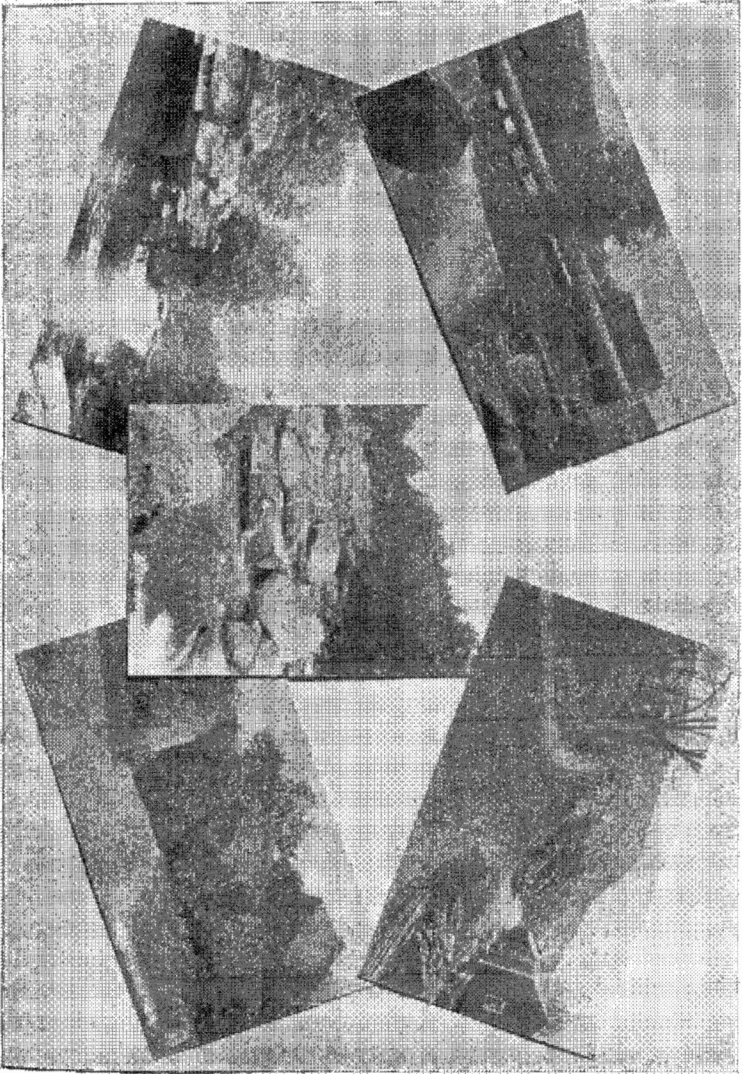

Scenes Near Bristol.

Lamoille River between Milton and Colchester.
Winooski.

amassed princely fortunes, in plain violation of their instructions, of the royal order of 1767, and in fraud of the rights of the crown as well as of the public.

The policy of ignoring the New Hampshire charters was begun by Cadwallader Colden, lieutenant-governor, who became the head of the government in August, 1761, and so continued until November, 1765, except a year when Gen. Monkton was governor. Sir Henry Moore was governor from November, 1765, to September, 1769, when he died, and Colden again came into power until succeeded by Lord Dunmore, October, 1770. Dunmore ruled until the arrival of his successor, Sir William Tryon in July, 1771. Tryon was thence governor until the breaking out of the Revolution, save that he was called to England, to explain his misdeeds in respect to these land grants, and was gone from April, 1774, to July, 1775, during which period Colden again acted as governor. Leaving out Gen. Monkton, these four other royal governors were of varying degrees of merit or demerit in the other functions of their office, but in their dealings with the people and the lands of the New Hampshire grants, they were precisely alike—each in his turn showed himself a cool, deliberate, grasping, avaricious and arrogant scoundrel. During the year ending in the accession of Dunmore in October, 1770, Colden had granted not less than 600,000 acres of government lands. Besides the enormous fees which he pocketed, he had contrived to reserve to himself, out of these grants, over 20,000 acres, and had provided liberally in lands for the several members of his family. Dunmore, another hungry Scotchman, made all haste to set himself under this shower of gold. Colden, to elude him, rushed his patents through the office, after the date of Dunmore's commission; and from that date till Dunmore ousted him, Colden bagged fees to the value of $25,000. The hungry Dunmore procured from Lord Hillsborough, colonial secretary, an order directing Colden to pay him, Dunmore, one half of these last stealings. Colden declined and applied by letter to Lord Hillsborough to reverse the order. Thereupon Dunmore caused a suit in the name of the king, to be instituted before himself as chancellor, for the recovery of this fund for his own benefit. "He had the shameless effrontery to hear the case solemnly argued by counsel and to prepare for deciding it in his own favor, but after one or two postponements of the time which he had fixed for that purpose, finding that his decree would be appealed from to the King in council, where it was sure that the case would be dismissed, he finally left it undecided and fortunate Colden continued to pocket the money."—*Hall.*   "So were they all, all honorable men !"

During the eight months of his administration Dunmore had managed to grant to speculators 450,000 acres of Vermont lands and to receive the fees for the same, and also by his own grant to himself, in the names of others, to become proprietor of 51,000 acres more.   This grant (says Gov. Hall) will serve to show the cool, unblushing manner in which the instructions of the king were violated by the New York governors, and how readily their frauds on the public were countenanced and participated in by the officers of government and other prominent individuals.   The land was petitioned for by one Alexander McLure, in behalf of himself and fifty associates, not naming them, stating that there was a vacant tract of land near Otter Creek, of 51,000 acres, of which he and his associates were desirous of obtaining a patent "intending to cultivate and improve the same."   The application, being laid before the council and approved, a patent was issued to McLure and fifty other persons by name on the 8th day of July, 1771, the very day on which Dunmore surrendered his office to Tryon, his successor.   Five days afterward all the other patentees conveyed their shares to Dunmore, who in the name of the king had issued the patent to them.   Among the patentees who thus voluntarily united in this gigantic fraud, were Alexander Colden, son of Lieut.-Gov. Colden and surveyor-general of the province; Andrew Elliott, the receiver general; Hugh Wallace and Henry White, members of the council; Edward Foy, Dunmore's private secretary; Goldsbrow Banyar, clerk of the council and deputy secretary of the province; Hugh Gaine, the public printer; Whitehead Hicks, mayor of the city of New York; and a long list of land speculators holding patentents for from 15,000 to 100,000 acres each, among whom were Simon Metcalf, John Bowles, John Kelley, Crean Brush and James Duane.   The land described in the patent was situated in the present county of Addison, and was a tract some twelve or thirteen miles in length from north to south, by six or seven in width, lying principally on the east side of Otter Creek in the towns of Leicester, Salisbury, and Middlebury, embracing within its limits the lake which bears the name of the noble lord who was both grantor and grantee; but reaching across the creek into the towns of Whiting and Cornwall.

All the land included in the patent had been previously granted by New Hampshire.   The granting of the land, as has been seen, was prohibited by the king's order of July 24, 1767; and the grant being

At Montpelier.

thus made without the authority of the crown, was unquestionably void in law for that reason, and would have been declared so by any competent and impartial judicial tribunal having power to determine it. That Dunmore was well aware that the prohibitory order was still in force is apparent from several letters of his (preserved in the Colonial History of New York) to Lord Hillsborough, vainly asking to have it rescinded.

Sir William Tryon, who was described by Bancroft as "selfish Tryon who under a smooth exterior concealed the heart of a savage," succeeded Dunmore July 8, 1771. Between that date and April, 1774, when he was called to England, he had made grants within the prohibited territory of over 200,000 acres of land, a considerable portion of which had been previously granted by New Hampshire. He also provided himself with a township of over 32,000 acres, by the name of Norbury, situated in the present county of Washington in the vicinity of Calais and Worcester. The patent was dated April 14, 1772, and was issued to thirty-two individuals, among whom were his son-in-law, Edmund Fanning, Receiver-General Elliott, Secretary Banyar, James Duane, Col. John Reid, John Kelly, Crean Brush and other noted land speculators.

Tryon had special occasion to know the king's order which he thus deliberately violated. For the order of July, 1767, that there might be no excuse for disregarding it, or any doubt about its construction, was on the 7th of February, 1771, incorporated into the standing instructions of the king to his New York governors in the words following:

" 49th. Whereas we thought fit by our order in council of the 20th of July, 1764, to declare that the western banks of the River Connecticut, from where it enters the province of Massachusetts Bay as far north as the 45th degree of northern latitude should be the boundary between the provinces of New York and New Hampshire; and whereas we have further thought fit by our order in council of July 24, 1767, to declare that no part of the lands lying on the western side of the Connecticut, *within that district heretofore claimed by our province of New Hampshire*, should be granted until our further pleasure should be known concerning the same. It is therefore our will and pleasure that you do take effectual care for the observance of said order in council, *and that you do not upon pain of our highest displeasure, presume to make any grant whatever, or pass any warrant of survey of any part of the said lands*, until our further will and pleasure shall be signified to you concerning the same."

These instructions were laid before the New York council July 24, 1771, by Gov. Tryon himself, and entered on its minutes, as appears by the records preserved in the colonial history of New York. The specious plea made by some of his predecessors that the king's order of 1767 only applied to lands already granted by New Hampshire, was therefore not available to Tryon. Indeed, it was never honestly available to anybody, as the original order was perfectly clear to the contrary ; and these worthy governors in fact only used it for the purpose of enabling the camel to get his nose into the tent. Having begun to grant on this theory, they made no discrimination between lands patented and lands unpatented by New Hampshire. But Tryon had no shadow of a theory. The grants made by him were in cool and insolent defiance of the explicit and iterated orders of the king by whose authority and in whose name he pretended to act. Moreover, they were made when the controversy had so far advanced that the parties were almost at actual war, and when the attention of the British government was sharply directed to it by applications for relief by the settlers.

On the 4th of December, 1771, Lord Hillsborough wrote to Tryon asking for a full report " of the method of proceeding upon application for grants of land, in order that his majesty may be informed whether such method does or does not correspond with the letter and spirit of the royal instructions given for that purpose ; for if it should turn out that grants are made to persons by name who never personally appear at the council board, or who are not examined as to their ability to cultivate and improve the land they petition for, *and that the insertion of names in a patent under pretense of their being associates or co-partners is only a color for giving to any one person more than he is allowed by the king's instructions, it is an abuse of so gross and fraudulent a nature as deserves the severest reprehension, and it is highly necessary, both for the interests of the crown and for the dignity of his majesty's government that some effectual measures should be taken to put a stop to it.*"

Tryon's answer was dated April 11, 1772, and in it he states that it would be extremely difficult to prevent the application for lands "under borrowed names," and then undertakes to vindicate the policy of making such grants, thus : " I conceive it, my lord, good policy to lodge large tracts of land in the hands of gentlemen of weight and consideration. *They will naturally farm out their lands to tenants ; a method which will ever create subordination, and counterpoise, in some measure, the general leveling spirit that so much prevails in some of his majesty's governments.*"

Among The Flowers.

On The Hills.   Rochester and Lincoln.

This is good New York doctrine to this day.   And Gov. Tryon was so firmly convinced of its soundness that three days after so setting it down in his answer, he signed the grant of 32,000 acres to himself as above stated.

Resolved to make hay while the sun shone, Tryon, the next July (1772) attended a congress of Indians at the residence of Sir William Johnson, where he assented to the purchase by a few individuals from the Mohawks, of more than a million acres of their lands, and promised to issue patents for the same to the purchasers.   Gen. Philip Schuyler, in a private letter written the following September, states that Tryon's fees on this visit amounted to £22,000, and adds: "A large premium is offered by the land jobbers at New York to any ingenious artist who shall contrive a machine to waft them to the moon. Should Fergerson, Martin, or any eminent astronomer, report that they had discovered large vales of fine land in that luminary, I would apply to be a commissioner for granting the lands, if I knew to whom to apply for it."

On hearing of this proceeding of Tryon's, Lord Dartmouth, the new colonial secretary, under date of Nov. 4, 1772, wrote to him, saying that "the engrossing of lands on the Mohawk on pretence of purchases from the Indians had been repeatedly and justly complained of," and forbidding him to take any steps to confirm the purchases, until the Indian deeds were transmitted to him and "the king's pleasure signified thereupon."   Lord Dartmouth also complained of his conduct in granting lands "annexed to New York, by the determination of the boundary with New Hampshire," which, he says, makes it necessary for the board of trade to resume again the consideration of the whole subject.

On the 3d of December, 1772, the Board of Trade made a representation of the whole matter to the committee of the Privy Council, in which they submitted several propositions for the adjustment thereof. In this representation the board speak of the difficulties which had arisen from the disregard by the New York governors of the king's order of July, 1767, of "the great injury and oppression suffered by the settlers from the irregular conduct of the governor and council of New York, in granting warrants of survey for lands under their actual 'improvement,'" and of the exorbitant fees demanded on the granting of lands, which they say are by the ordinance of 1710 "considerably larger than what are at this day received for the same service in any other of the colonies," and yet, the representation proceeds, "the governor, the secretary, and the surveyor, have taken and do now ex-

act *more than double what that ordinance allows*, and a number of
other officers do upon various pretences take fees upon all grants of
land insomuch that the whole amount of these fees upon a grant of
one thousand acres of land, is in many instances not far short of the
real value of the fee simple; and we think we are justified in suppos-
ing that it has been from a consideration of the advantage arising from
these exorbitant fees, that his majesty's governors of New York have
of late years taken upon themselves, upon the most unwarrantable
pretences, to elude the restrictions contained in his majesty's instructions with regard to the quantity of land to be granted to any
one person, and to contrive by the insertion in one grant of a number
of names either fictitious or which if real, are only lent for the purpose, to convey to one person in one grant from twenty to forty
thousand acres of land, an abuse which is now grown to that height
as well to deserve your lordship's attention."

In a letter from Lord Dartmouth to Governor Tryon, dated the
9th of the same December, he says: "I am further to acquaint you
with the fact that the sentiments expressed in Lord Hillsborough's
letter to you of the 4th of December, 1771, concerning the unwarrantable and collusive practice of granting lands in general, are fully
adopted by the king's servants, and I was exceedingly surprised to
find that such an intimation to you on that subject had not had the
effect to restrain that practice; and that the same unjustifiable collu-
sion had been adopted in a still greater extent in the licenses you
have granted to purchase lands of the Indians." In a letter of March
3, 1773, Lord Dartmouth again expresses his dissatisfaction with the
conduct of Governor Tryon, in relation both to the licenses granted
to the purchasers of land from the Indians, and to the patenting of
lands covered by grants under New Hampshire.

The report of the Board of Trade of December 3, 1772, before
mentioned, having been approved by the king in council, was transmitted to Governor Tryon, with instructions to have it carried into
effect; and he, in reply, addressed a long communication to the colonial secretary, insisting that the plan therein proposed was unjust to
the New York patentees and impracticable. He also, in another letter, attempted a defence of his conduct in relation to the purchases
of the lands of the Indians. In reply to this last letter Lord Dartmouth, under date of the 4th of August, 1773, says: "I have read
and considered your letter with great attention, and still remain of
opinion, that a license given without the king's previous consent and
instruction, to private persons to make purchases from the Indians

College Girls.

of above a million of acres of land, accompanied with an engagement to confirm their titles by letters patent under the seal of the colony, was contrary to the plain intention of the royal proclamation of 1763, incompatible with the spirit of the king's instructions, and an improper exercise of the power of granting lands, vested in the governor and council."

Lord Dartmouth further declares that he cannot advise the king to confirm the purchases, but intimates that the purchasers may perhaps be entitled to some reasonable compensation for their expenses; and he then adds, "but I must be better informed of many circumstances before I can judge in what mode it can be given; and it is for this reason, as well as from a consideration of the want of a more ample and precise explanation of the state of the province in general respecting those different claims to lands that have been a source of so much disquiet and disorder, that I have humbly moved the king that you may be directed to come for a short time to England, and his majesty has been graciously pleased to approve thereof."

The receipt of this letter was acknowledged by Tryon early in October, but as it allowed him considerable latitude in regard to the time of his departure, he postponed it until the ensuing spring.

When the New York assembly met in January, 1764, Tryon, in announcing to them his call to England, thoughtfully suppressed the fact that it was to account for his own rascalities, and kindly laid the blame upon the settlers of the grants, as follows : "The contests which have arisen between the New York grantees and the claimants under New Hampshire, and the outrages committed on the settlers under this government, having been productive of much confusion and disorder, and requiring immediate consideration, his majesty has been graciously pleased to command me to repair to England for a short time to attend to the discussion of this important matter."

Tryon was gone from April 7, 1774, to July, 1775, during which time as we have seen, the thrifty Colden in defiance of all these instructions granted 400,000 acres of Vermont lands by patents, which, being without authority, were utterly null and void. These raps which Tryon got from the home government, though concealed from the settlers, doubtless accounted in a large degree for the conciliatory policy adopted by him toward them about that time as we shall see later. When he arrived in England, the kingdom was shaken by the throes of the coming American Revolution, and but little attention seems to have been paid to his case. It was, however, in March,

1775, agreed in the Board of Trade that a case should be stated relative to the conflicting grants and brought by appeal before the king and his privy council. But Col. Reid, who held a grant of 7,000 acres, made in violation of the order of 1767, and who was also agent for Lord Dumore in relation to his grant to himself, appeared and alleged that he had material evidence to submit to the Board, and thereby procured a reconsideration of this vote. The war intervened and the matter was carried no further. It would seem that Tryon, Reid and Dunmore all had the best of reasons for not desiring to have their doings tested by judicial proceedings. Tryon returned to New York to find the country involved in civil war. He remained in New York city from July to October, relying upon James Duane, then a member the continental congress, for notice when he must leave to avoid arrest. Such notice came early in October, and he escaped to a British man of war in the harbor. After this, pursuant to his chronic habit of violating the king's orders, he issued a patent, October 28, 1775, to Samuel Avery and others for 40,000 acres west of the Green mountains, and another, in June, 1776, to Samuel Holland and others for 23,000 acres east of the same. These facts are mostly taken from Hall's Early History of Vermont.

In the mean time the New York government repassed the annulled act creating Cumberland county in 1768, and in 1770 erected into a county, by the name of Gloucester the territory lying north of Cumberland county and east of the Green mountains, fixing the county seat at Newbury. All that part of Vermont on the west side of the mountains not included in Charlotte county was made part of the county of Albany with county seat at Albany, New York. The success attending Mr. Robinson's mission, although it failed to stop the usurpations of New York, yet inspired the settlers with complete confidence in the legality as well as the justice of their claims, and gave them strong hope that their rights would sooner or later be protected by the Crown.

[*To be continued.*]

At South Hero.

Mountain Road in Autumn. Granville.

Mountain Stream, Ripton.   At Lake Pl'iad.
A Green Mountain Girl.
At Middlebury.   On The Road in Hancock.

No other state in the Union has a Fire Insurance Company
with so grand a record as Vermont.

THE - - -

VERMONT MUTUAL

FIRE INSURANCE CO.

OF MONTPELIER,

WITH SEVENTY YEARS EXPERIENCE, AND

$3,697,548.00

FOR THE PAYMENT OF LOSSES.

Two-thirds of the VOTING POPULATION of the State
are members and policy holders.

Every property owner in Vermont should secure a policy in
this old, reliable State Company, and so get his
insurance at the lowest possible cost.

AN AGENT IN EVERY TOWN.

FRED. E. SMITH, President.

JAMES T. SABIN, Secretary,

WM. T. DEWEY, Treasurer.

The Cause and Effect

www.ingramcontent.com/pod-product-compliance
Lightning Source LLC
Chambersburg PA
CBHW031452270326
41930CB00007B/955